Jackie Robinson

Karen Davila

Boston, Massachusetts
Chandler, Arizona
Glenview, Illinois
Upper Saddle River, New Jersey

Illustrations
All illustrations: London Ladd.

ISBN-13: 978-0-328-67562-3
ISBN-10:   0-328-67562-8

4 5 6   V0FL 16 15 14 13 12

Jackie Robinson loved sports.

He played on teams in school.

He was a **champion** jumper.

Later he wanted to play baseball.

Baseball teams were not fair.

They had no African Americans.

One team took a big step.

That team let Robinson play.

Some people tried to stop him.
Robinson had to try even harder.

Robinson led the way for others.

He was a real champion!

Glossary

champion someone who is
   the best at something